Miracle Maker

الأسد والحواري

وإذا كنتَ حوارياً منقوشاً راسمُه في لوح الشهداء
فأنا الأسدُ الضانك أربضُ قدامك في الحلبة
إعلم ما شئتَ بجناتِ الفردوسي
فيما أنا أُمنشي أوصالك حتى العظم
آه، لذ تلعني أنتَ العارف أنا نحن الإثنين
سنؤدّي واجبنا المكتوب علينا في هذا العالم
متحدين
فاصعدْ فرحاً منتصراً نحو سماءِ الخلد
فيما نحن أُسودَ الغابة
سنظلُّ نزمجرُ فوق الدرجِ هنا
حتى نرضي الشيّيين.

فاضل العزاوي

Miracle Maker

Selected Poems of

Fadhil Al-Azzawi

Translated from the Arabic by
Khaled Mattawa

BOA Editions, Ltd. ∽ Rochester, NY ∽ 2003

First Edition

Publications by BOA Editions, Ltd.—
a not-for-profit corporation under section 501 (c) (3)
of the United States Internal Revenue Code—
are made possible with the assistance of grants from
the Literature Program of the New York State Council on the Arts,
the Literature Program of the National Endowment for the Arts,
the Sonia Raiziss Giop Charitable Foundation,
the Lannan Foundation,
as well as from the Mary S. Mulligan Charitable Trust,
the County of Monroe, NY,
and the Ames-Amzalak Memorial Trust.

Cover Design: Daphne Poulin-Stofer
Cover Photograph: "Untitled" by Salima Salih, courtesy of the photographer.
Interior Design and Composition: Richard Foerster
BOA Logo: Mirko

LIBRARY OF CONGRESS CATALOGING-IN-PUBLICATION DATA

Azzawi, Fadil.
   [Poems. English. Selections]
   Miracle maker : selected poems / Fadhil Al-Azzawi ; translated from the Arabic by
Khaled Mattawa.
   p. cm. — (The Lannan translations selection series)
   ISBN 1-929918-44-5 (cloth : alk. paper) — ISBN 1-929918-45-3 (pbk. : alk. paper)
   1. Azzawi, Fadil—Translations into English. I. Mattawa, Khaled. II. Title. III.
Series.

PJ7814.Z92A25 2003
892.7'16—dc22   2003055872

BOA Editions, Ltd.
Thom Ward, Editor
H. Allen Spencer, Chair
A. Poulin, Jr., President & Founder (1938–1996)
260 East Avenue, Rochester, NY 14604
www.boaeditions.org

CONTENTS

☙❧

from *Rising to the Spring* (1960–1974)

☙❧

from *The Eastern Tree* (1975)

∞∞

from *A Man Throws Stones into a Well* (1978-1988)

∞∞

from *At The End of All Journeys* (1994)

∞∞

from *A Moth on Its Way to Fire* (1998)

from *Bedouins Under an Alien Sky* (2002)

THE MAKING OF A MIRACLE MAKER

In the aftermath of a violent 1963 coup in Iraq that brought Baath-affiliated officers to power, Fadhil Al-Azzawi was among the thousands of intellectuals and political activists thrown into the notorious Al-Hilla prison. The facility became quickly overcrowded, and the administrators decided to make the gallows room their sorting house. Many stories began to circulate about the fate of prisoners who were ushered into that ominous room. It was whispered that it had been the recent site of the execution of twenty men and women. Al-Azzawi, who was twenty-four at the time, recounts that a quiet sense of panic began to spread among the prisoners.

Yet, the prisoners tried to accommodate themselves with the space allotted them. The gallows hole, through which the hanged body would fall, was covered with a wooden board. Prisoners made their bedding around *the board*, some claiming, unconvincingly, that it would break under their weight. Eventually, someone lifted the board and looked. Later, a few inmates went into the hole to see how the apparatus worked. One prisoner mimicked the shudders and the stiff body of a hanged man, making his fellow inmates laugh. There were some athletes in the room, possibly gymnasts, who gripped a metal pole inside the hole and began to perform acrobatic movements that thrilled and entertained their fellow prisoners.

Al-Azzawi's memoir *Al-Rouh Al-Haya (The Living Spirit)*, in which this experience is recounted, also includes a long chapter devoted to the various torturers he and his fellow prisoners endured. One torturer used to ask his captives to choose the methods of pain they wished to have performed on them. Another sang softly to his victims during breaks between sessions. The same man told his victim a series of hilarious jokes before beginning his regimen. A third offered his victims glasses of arak before torturing them. "It will numb your nerves a bit," he would say to a victim.

These disturbing memories drive a good share of Al-Azzawi's poetic investigation. The torturer is as pitiful as his victim, and the line between heroism and delusion is thinner than we are willing to admit. Al-Azzawi's poems do not merely remind us of the existence of such realities; they document the poet's miraculous effort to overcome them.

Fadhil Al-Azzawi was born in 1940 in Kirkuk, a multiethnic, multisectarian, and multilingual city in northern Iraq. As a child he heard Turkoman poets reciting poems they spontaneously composed on their way home after a night of drinking. The following morning, the best lines from these impromptu compositions were recited among the people in the marketplace. At a Quranic school, he memorized chapters of the Quran, internalized their sonorities and deep rhythms. Al-Azzawi also witnessed Sufi performances of dancing and religious incantations. Piercing their bodies with swords and knives, pulling them out without spilling a drop of blood, dervishes demonstrated the invulnerable state of their communion with the divine. To such exposure we may attribute our poet's interest in the carnivalesque.

While still in his teens, Al-Azzawi published his first poems in the late 1950s in such important Beirut-based venues as *al-Adab* and *Shiir*. Assuming the editors might withhold publication of his poems if they knew his true age, he kept that information to himself. In 1958 he entered Baghdad University and soon after joined the Iraqi Communist Party. Three years later, in 1961, he publicly resigned from the ICP condemning the party for dictatorial practices and for limiting its members' freedom of expression. Working as a freelance editor and journalist, and unprotected by the ICP, Al-Azzawi was thrown into jail twice for his published writings.

In 1963, after the Baathist coup, he was sentenced to three years in jail on trumped-up charges and was summarily expelled from the university. During his prison term he smuggled out some of his poems, and, subsequently, they were published in major Arab periodicals. In 1965 he was released and all charges against him were dismissed. He now began working as an editor for several important Iraqi daily newspapers while translating numerous works of international literature and criticism. He also reenrolled in Baghdad University and completed the requirements for a bachelor's degree in English.

During the more tolerant years that followed his release from prison, Al-Azzawi helped form a group that became known as the Sixties Generation, the nucleus of which was an earlier collection of poets called the Kirkuk Group. In a manifesto released in 1969, Al-Azzawi and other members of the Sixties Generation declare,

The good poet, even when he is being political, attempts to look at things as if he is seeing them for the first time, as if they are being created by his own hands. . . . The world of poetry is not only this visible world that is dominated by logical rules. The world of poetry contains the visible world, the invisible world, the personal world, and the world of other generations and eras.

The Sixties Generation poets engaged in politics and openly protested the antidemocratic measures of the Iraqi government. Similarly, they insisted that poetry attempt to reach deeper states of imaginative reflection. They were just as interested in social justice as in metaphysics and the subconscious. All practices that enabled people to break through the limits imposed on their lives were worthy of exploration and effort. And poetry was one of these practices.

In the early 1970s the Baathists consolidated their hold on power, and the government became increasingly hostile to dissent. Several of the magazines and literary journals Al-Azzawi worked for were shut down, their publications confiscated. His attempts to regroup the Union of Iraqi Writers were thwarted. A boisterous recitation of one of his protest poems before a large audience landed him in jail for a few days. Sixties Generation poets began to leave the country. In 1976 Al-Azzawi accepted a scholarship for doctoral work in communication sciences at the University of Leipzig in East Germany. Twenty-seven years later neither he nor his wife Salima Salih have returned to Iraq.

During Al-Azzawi's childhood Iraq was under British mandate, ruled by a monarchy that served the oil interests of Great Britain. All the while various indigenous political factions were vying for influence and vowing to replace the monarchy. The people demanded national independence, democracy, land reform, and a just distribution of the new oil revenues. Poets such as the formalist Muhammad Al-Jawahiri and modernist Badr Shakir Al-Sayyab were at the forefront of this struggle. The powerful poetry they wrote and recited expressed their nation's unrequited longings.

We see this spirit of protest throughout Al-Azzawi's poetry. Early on he was clearly aware of the oppressive institutional and cultural forces suffocating his country. Unfortunately, these forces did not become dismantled after the 1958 "revolution" that toppled the monarchy in a bloody, but highly popular coup. The military junta that ruled after the revolution became more repressive than the monarchy it replaced. It was Al-Azzawi's disillusionment with the new regime that led to his first stint in jail. The clown in the first poem in this volume, *sings / sings / while little / by little / the star dies out*. In the second poem, an elderly Romeo is unfazed by opposition to his views. He states, *I am the prophet of passion. This is my confession. / Let the boys laugh at me*. The poem that follows, "Prisoner No. 907," presents a speaker defiant to the bitter end.

The poems cited above are among Al-Azzawi's more personal and less directly political works. In these early poems, a young poet's poems if you will, we find an intentional twining of the themes of love and freedom. If one could love freely, the poems seem to argue, one is living freely. And if one lives freely, he or she will find love. Clearly prisoner No. 907 was not thrown in jail because he falls *in love with foolish girls / and the women of the university*. His opposition to those in power is linked to his desire for love, and he aims to have both or nothing.

∞∞

It is difficult to ascertain how prison affected Al-Azzawi, his writing process, and his philosophical outlook. Before being incarcerated he fully enjoyed his life as a poet and writer. After his two years in jail he resumed his literary career with the same energy as before. However, new and bold strategies began to appear in his poetry. We begin to encounter Al-Azzawi's comic sensibility with greater regularity. Elements of the surreal and fabulous become major motifs in his work. And most importantly, he becomes more experimental, starts to employ multitonality, nonlinearity, and the non sequitur in his poems.

All of these changes appear in the marvelous poem "The Teachings of F. Al-Azzawi to the World". The poem's broad canvas—multitonality, metapoetic gestures, and nonlinearity—showcases Al-Azzawi's revitalized poetics and political vision. By achieving poetic unity through juxtaposed forms, the poem creates a counter-discourse to any kind of monologic or linear discourse, becomes a kind of democracy full of contradictions and retractions. But the poet's voice never gets lost in the cacophony he creates.

In *The Eastern Tree*, published in 1975, Al-Azzawi adopts the fable and finds it a useful trope for rendering contemporary concerns. While humor and realism are never out of reach in this book-length sequence, a sense of isolation dominates the poems. Abdullah, the protagonist, seems aware of human potential and experience, but the world keeps forcing him back to square one. In these poems we leave the Iraqi political scene, and, possibly, the world we know altogether. Abdullah, a name meaning "servant of God," speaks for every man. His unplanned, picaresque journey leads him, at one turn, to be crowned as a king and, in another instance, to pull the plow like a beast of burden. Prophet and clown, sage and nave, Abdullah attempts to know the world as it is without utopian hopes or presumptions. Not yet an exile, Al-Azzawi, it seems, was rehearsing for a life of detachment, one that is deeply in touch with its hopes and desires, but far from achieving them. *The Eastern Tree* was the last poetry book Al-Azzawi published in Iraq.

◕—◖

Upon moving to Germany, Al-Azzawi chose to employ a kind of postapocalyptic fable as the basic setting for his new poems. Undoubtedly, this inclination was influenced by the Iran-Iraq war and by the general sociopolitical regression permeating the Arab world. In his work from the 1980s, we see the frenzy of the alchemist mixing elements to reach an unknown ideal. In poems such as "No Matter How Far," "The Last Iraq," and "Memory," the sentences seem burdened by what they contain while accelerating the horror of the drama they depict. Al-Azzawi's fables proceed in constant tension with reality; they are not created to *help us* escape our lived experiences, but to heighten our awareness of the potential dangers that surround us.

Exile also forced Al-Azzawi to examine his particular isolation through the dual lenses of memory and attachment to his native country. Poems such as "A Man in Memory" narrate what seem to be autobiographical experiences. Poignantly, this heartbreaking narrative examines the possibility of redemption under a corrupt and repressive regime. The repetition and refrain in "Song of Myself" rise with the speaker's hopes and crash as these hopes come tumbling down. At the end of each decade of his life, the speaker collects his bearings and again convinces himself, *Everything will be all right, Fadhil.* But when the speaker reaches fifty, he brings the cycle of hope and disappointment to a halt. "Leave me alone, damn it!" he says. And we, like the poet, are left wondering how so much time has passed without learning a thing.

One major statement of protest in *The End of All Journeys* is "Elegy for the Living," written on the eve of the first American war on Iraq. In its formal structure the poem is reminiscent of "The Teachings of F. Al-Azzawi to the World." Here the fablesque serves our poet, to use Gabriel Garcìa-M·rquez's words, as "an unconventional means to render an unconventional existence." The speaker sees the war explode before him and envisions his country being incinerated. His historical awareness leads him to conclude that this war is no different from Hulago's sacking of Baghdad in the thirteenth century. The American war on Iraq, he determines, registers the failure of North American civilization. To Al-Azzawi, the enterprise that has given us Hemingway and Ginsberg, Elvis Presley and Marilyn Monroe has come to this:

> capitalism sits
> in her old carriage
> greeting the crowds lining the streets
> on her way to hell.

Pointing out U.S. imperialism as an enemy of progress engenders no hope for victory, resistance, or solidarity. Iraq is spent. The bombs fall and murder the innocent, murder prisoners of Saddam Hussein's bloody regime, murder *mothers pondering their distant children / planting their trees in exile*. It is a scene of devastation, an apocalypse where there is no escape, no victory for the forces of good and decency. Writing from exile, the poet can only call upon death to *come and take us on a stretcher / and raise us to eternity*.

Exile, in Al-Azzawi's work, becomes a kind of perpetual fable from which the poet cannot escape. A theater in a train station plays a movie that never ends. Night soldiers frighten the child; he pleads with them to go away, but they never speak to him, and they never go away. Even the traditions that were a source of delight for Al-Azzawi become a target of his satirical wit. The cast of Quranic characters, including God, are scrutinized and mocked. In "Good Morning, God" Al-Azzawi chides his highly personalized God for not stopping by to visit him in his apartment in Berlin. The miracle of Abraham's survival from his kinsmen's fire, Joseph's picaresque life story, and the journey of the three Magi, all are projected through the poet's tragicomic vision.

And though events are stark in Al-Azzawi's world, the poet's spirit is not daunted. His elegy for the Russian revolution and his exuberant poem

"Toasts" are defenses for his idealism. Perhaps one of the unintended benefits of exile is that the poet's voice becomes more personable, more forgiving, even as it is more bitter. Gone is the voice of the poet ready to launch himself into myth, the voice that anticipates action as an echo of his words, a spirit upon whom everything depends. Calmer, steadier, the older Al-Azzawi makes us laugh and even pity the utter ignorance of the forces that oppress us. In poem after poem Al-Azzawi breaks down political repression, pride and self-loathing, stupidity and greed, all that shackles the human spirit. With the world's tight strictures loosened by his sense of humor, his wide-ranging knowledge, his patience with our follies and absurdities, and the joy his language provides, the closer we get to the personal realm of Fadhil Al-Azzawi, the bigger that world becomes. It is a miracle Al-Azzawi has for decades performed.

—KM

Miracle Maker

from *Rising to the Spring*

(1960–1974)

THE CLOWN AND THE DANCER

Wine in the cups
and he sings the blaze of the forests
in her eyes.
Dancer of the tavern
you are a step in a blind man's night.
You are a step.
You are
      blind.
Don't ask me. I love everyone,
but my lover is a matchless saint.
The stage is ablaze with dance,
and the tear is put out in a story
told by a drunk lover
who sings
sings
while little
by little
the star dies out.

ROMEO IN OLD AGE

Flame of sixty years,
if I wept nightly over my loss
who will water my tears?
Who will raise life out of death?
Who will believe me if I said, "Flowers
grow and laugh on my banks"?
I am the prophet of passion. This is my confession.
Let the boys laugh at me:
      Romeo without Juliet,
      O Juliet relent.
      Dear God, inspire her
      for you are the sun in the night
      of the old and spent.

A retired man who is not good at chess
spends his nights swearing by the stars,
but the night star has set.

PRISONER NO. 907

In my cell the clock of my days
stops. I enter its darkness like a banished king
who stays up at night's gate.
I fall in love with foolish girls
and the women of the university
who love with the silence of children
and the pain of prisoners.
In my cell
I seek a moment of love
on the face of the world.

THE BUDDHIST'S MASKS

The Buddhist's face is before me
eyeing the moment of crisis
between the subject and the verb.
If the names of freedom
glitter before the fighter's face,
if night illuminates the shore,
if love is a friend left in exile,
let us bow to this age melting among the ages
where the past and the present shiver
in the house of the future, and sadness
hunts murdered dreams
on the day rising through the night of man.

If full-throated poetry is to be sentenced
in the brass market, then the meaning of meaning
is not to exist.

The window is cracked open by the wind.
I creep among the faces, search for a man
who bet on my head in the battle of silence, and who tore the masks of
          the ancestors
off my face. He departed without leaving an address.
On the lips of the lover there is a tired song
about a prophet who died in prison.

Returning from a dance, Night
listens to the mermaids' music
while an old man looks for a bottle of wine.
In a hurricane of silver voices
I talk about cubist poetry:
a knock on the door, and at the window is the blacksmith's wife
listening languidly
to the worries of poets and readers.
The torturer, the torturer, the torturer,
a time stamped with damnation

on the forehead of an apostate priest.
This wisdom was in your market, Tashkent.
But I did not seek it.

On 6/7/2000
Love abdicates words
and the shore will stop dispatching the dead:
Who will convince me now to be silent?
to hang this voice?—
to throw away this imposed history?
Nothing will come except death.
I will gamble the world away, even for a slap
that wipes the tears off my eyelashes.

On 6/7/2000
The day will have spring in its eyes
and Night will be the end of night.
Poets of damnation, eat the mystery of the future while people stand
          around in the dark,
for in the slave market wisdom has torn away
the dragon's skin,
and the atheist now longs for Paradise.

On this day: Saturday
in this mild month: March,
in this year: the sixty-fifth,
in this room in a closed house,
on this street in Batawiyeen,
the crisis is:
          to end this stanza,
          to take up silence.

MR. EDOUARD LUQA'S DILEMMA

The legend is persecuted in the book of creation.
The tourist takes up selling leather masks.
The one-eyed king in his collapsed balcony
deliberates invading the Hittites.
The chapter ends with a laugh—Jean Genet's.
The students at the institute gossip about a director with a limp.
She colors her cheeks with rouge, and in her laugh glow the rules of
       correct pronunciation,
which thoroughly embarrasses the janitors at the department of music.
Mr. Edouard Luqa crosses over to
al-Khalanni bookshop,
but he has failed the rules of rhetoric.

In Hotel Zeya the Orientalist forgets
his wife, drinks apple wine at the bar,
wearing a hat of stringy straw.
The summer oppresses Agatha Christie as she writes
her detective novel on Babel.
In the third act of the comedy of errors
the heroes suffer and the thieves die.
The beggars of Baghdad learn to dance
at the Oberge nightclub.

O face of Judas Iscariot,
give your features some meaning.
People clobber one another before the altar
while I watch from my doorstep.
I hunt eagles to embalm
and think about killing someone who's not yet born.

In meter, the thought taps the head of the poet.
He goes to the market and brings the proverbial golden scale.
He memorizes metrical feet in the students' café,
spits on wisdom, shies from *faalan, mafulan, faalan,*
tweezes the twisted sounds

from the judge's throat.
He writes two lines of poetry, lights the abyss
in the face of the ninth man, switches on his genie-mule
with a whip, and leaves like a chameleon.

Love	Game
Poetry	Lie
Man	Whore

all celebrate tonight at the International Club of Humanity.

So that poetry tears out the masks of convention,
so that the word encompasses the world,
I am crucified in this exile
outside the guidelines of the profession
flogging the faces of the poets.

A BELL

Standing
under the edge
of my night, I see the sea,
a table set for the birds,
a pagan lover facing the shores
writing on the beautiful water
his Babylonian name.
Come to me. I am a language for weeping,
an afternoon of walking above the evening
toward new people.
The sea takes its coins from me and writes my name:
a prince who leaves at night on the ships of distant wars.
Come, come, come
to me.
Come, come, come
to me.

THE TEACHINGS OF F. AL-AZZAWI

1

I lit my father's boat and rode the wave
rising along the shore of my joy,
ascending the path of revolution.
I saw borders torn down (as my soul aimed for
the valley of understanding
phantoms from drowned cities accompanied me
through white night). I cried, "Let me escape
from this body laid out like a signpost."
But the desert saw me, followed me like a serpent,
and I ran toward another kingdom
and saw the sea.

2

This is how I came upon burning streets, storefronts shut in the face of
        protests demanding bread and work.
I saw tanks rolling past driven by poor soldiers armed with machine guns.
I saw the enemies' planes climbing the shoulder of the homeland
dousing us with tons of manifestoes, dynamite, and chocolate.
That's why I sat facing the garden of love and thought
children can die without disease,
and that war commands its friends to oppress God—our sole ally who
        sits forever on the edge of the universe/ throwing us his
        teachings: opium for free.
And that is why
I am grateful,
for drugs are expensive these days, and there is nothing to get one excited
        except poems recited in raucous bars with a bunch of friends
        conquering the night.

In this age, as memories later become history
taught at elementary schools (sixth grade specifically),

I abducted, just for fun, a policeman from the year 1967 and washed
        him with soap and Dettol
for a whole month
then planted him in the garden of the homeland,
but he remained a dead tree forever.
In the morning when I passed by him I used to say: "When are you
        going to flower, dear policeman?"
"Not now, at least, not now."
And when he died I cried a great deal
for he was vaster than my homeland.

3

I'm not allowed to write my names,
        to elegize my generation,
        to kidnap the devil from God's capital.
I'm not allowed to dream that I'm dreaming,
        to sit like a blind man and travel the world in an ambulance,

or think that I am:
        a man hung in the courtyard of his house,

or think that I am:
        a man without any particular attributes, a man in the kingdom
            of the unknown
who cries, "This is my voice,"
and the sound dries on his lips
and death itself dies—
        (to see, to write, to witness).
I'm not allowed to sit alone on a sidewalk and weep out my sadness.
I'm not allowed to go into a toilet and contemplate the future.
I'm not allowed to dream that I am F. Al-Azzawi,
            that I'm a murdered chair,
            that I am my nation.

That is why I will now kidnap a bearded priest from a refugee camp
and travel the blood of the condemned
toward the mirrors of the soul—
(this is my voice).

4

Once as night walked shadowing a forest,
I heard a Bedouin say, "I am a tree."
I said, "How could that be when you're returning from June for the
        third time?"
He said, "Come with me!"
We traveled toward night in a cart
and I heard the saints declare,
"Martyrs are barred from the world
except in states of emergency
and during night battles."

5

Why?
Why? Why?
Why? Why? Why?
Why? Why? Why? Why?
Why? Why? Why?
Why? Why?
Why?

How did you fall when you were the sky shading the victim's face?
Why did you stand staring at those staring at the night?
You were a cry in my body, and you were a cause.
You were my question. That is why I reached for your lighthouse and
        gave you my secret.
I thought you filled the earth with me, and that with me truth stands
        upright,
and that my death, my happiness, rises from the darkness of prisons.
I thought of the masses rolled over by conquerors,
and I thought I was a garden.

Come to my country and loot it.
Come to my country, share with us our starvation.
Eat our bitter bread, O prophets of Zion.
Eat my blood, O Indian pilgrims.

Eat, O Persians, from the flesh of my people.
Borders have fallen from my borders.
Come to my country and kill it.
Come to my body and tread upon it,
for I was once a garden.

6

Because I am a cloud raining on the funeral of the sea,
I sit on the moment between heresy and the wind,
on the thrones of cities while the plague saves his coins
to buy up my country. I witness all the world's statues
coming down the street and sleeping with children
so that a new generation is born without any redeeming qualities
whose dreams are warmed by schizophrenia.

For this, and for other than this, and so that we do not forgo our claim
        in another era,
I decided to write this letter to my own head:
Remain a stranger
while fighters from a thousand directions traverse you
and, as the sea, free of intentions, calls out to the sand that is my
        country,
to subdue the foam that swirls the circles of time
where happiness smokes the wretchedness of the poor
and where the wise men write about
        the manufacture of birds,
        the proletariat in new happy cities,
        man without limbs,
        and the civilization of love.

                Hello Fadhil al-Azzawi,
                I'm talking to you from the precipice of time
                filled with fish, corpses, and pins
                and where there is no tunnel.
                Let's go to De Gaulle and talk to him about May 1968.
                Let's go to the generals of Greece and listen to
                        Zorba's music.

Let's go to Nassiteon as he devours communists.
Let's go to Amman and look into all the other Arab
capitals.
Let's go to some prison and talk to it about the other
prisons.
Let's go to no place at all.

7

At dawn I rose and saw closed-up alleys and springs gushing from a
desert.
I beheld the birds of the forest.
I gave children the sciences of revolution.
I left the rivers behind me,
a lover smuggled in the era of the masses,
and I heard the trees sing
to the night.
I heard man suffer loneliness among the people,
and the sea unite his children with the wind.
Homeland poured on the sadness of the East,
tell me:
how can flight happen without wings?
How could there be death without a birth certificate?
And on the sidewalks of dreams,
how can your birds abandon the forests of the heart?

8

Look at this man:

I know he will die on one of these days:
Saturday, Sunday, Monday, Tuesday, Wednesday, Thursday, Friday.
Or in one of these months:

January, February, March, April, May, June, July, August, September, October, November, December.
Look at him. He is writing poems so as not to die on the days of the week or the months of the year.

Note: to abbreviate this section I request that readers scrap it and just write the day and the month in which I will die (after my death of course) instead of having to write all the days of the week and the months of the year.

9

Manifesto Issued from the Last Trench of the Revolution

Fight with us for a happier world
Free hotel rooms
Come sleep with us on collective beds

A world revolution in cities and countryside to create the Corporation of Free Society (Dh. M. M. Inc.), we declare we will fight for the following goals:

1.
2.
3.
4.

Fill in the blanks with whatever goals you wish. We trust you.

Signed:
The Old Committee for the New Revolution

10

Large as a tree, a torturer with a shaved head led me to the court of an Abbassid sultan whose name I can't recall (maybe he had no name at all). Stroking his beard, the sultan asked me politely to create a plane for him with which to attack his enemies gathered in Khurasan.

But I refused his request (what do you expect from me? I am against wars that offer me nothing). I don't know how the sultan learned that I excelled at making jet fighters.

The sultan said, "Do you refuse then?"

I said, "An airplane? What an insolent Bedouin you are! Go ride a camel. As long as you don't know who Einstein was, you'll never ride an airplane. And how did you learn about airplanes in the first place? That's hilarious.

The torturer struck the back of my neck with his strong fist and I fell to my knees. Still, the sultan cowered before me and said coyly, "Fine, I'll gather all the jurists, men of letters, and poets, and I'll ask them to find out about the man you mentioned. What's his name? Ah, Einstein. He's a non-Arab. In a day, I'll bring you his family tree. But why do you care about this man?"

I answered, "Because he was better than me at making airplanes. But he escaped with my favorite neighbor. She was a Circassian, and they rode an Australian mule and went to an unknown country."

The sultan raved and ranted and looked disturbed. "What a filthy dog, betrayer of trust!" he said.

He issued an edict and the police went out in jet-black night looking for the wise traitor and great scientist.

The wise men, poets, and men of letters began digging through their books for his ancestors, all the way to Noah. It would be unthinkable that he would not have been on Noah's ark. Therefore it would be impossible to locate him among those who lived on earth before that time.

11

I want to leave the bottle of the soul and visit Baghdad at night, to see its phantoms wailing in alleyways open to sadness and storms that blow from the shores of history. What did the days say on their leisurely walks? Which desert is having a celebration? Here pain is a new language roaming from continent to continent. I try to leave my ash-existence. You are a country of yes and no/ Come closer/ Of an eternal spider under a thousand moons crawling from traps set for storms/ Beware!/ I see a city rising behind a river, and from the limbs of villages that call out, "This is a time when love is murdered," where feudalism emerges from its fields smeared with the syphilis of peace, where death is a ledger in which a man who is dissolving writes, "There is no limit to life, and death is the way." Don't die, I am your friend, O death, and I have come. My desire for life has set my blood on fire. The female rhinoceros is roaming a forest raised by the crucified master in his last supper, but the newspapers of the left and the right ignored his sermon, not mentioning him even in a corner of their crime pages. Sand under my feet, and winter crosses nature and the seasons scream, "I am blind and cannot see a thing." Has dawn left the mountains with the curse of war on his hands? Or is he riding the mule of justice wandering among the villages?—visiting prisons and brothels to become a king, or a senator, or a gambler sitting in the cave of his days, not saying what the stranger says in his holy books.

12

Lift the curtain, you will find a man facing the rivers as they pour into
    each other.
He stares from the spear's launching point at his shoulder
and sees nothing except a building leaning toward the sidewalk,
but as night releases its dogs
the song sings its song to the end
and the chairs of the dead recline to the sentiments of the masses.
It's better to think of the rivers later
(because rivers are like Assyrians who become alienated whenever they
    visit their homeland)
as they carry off the poorest soldiers to freedom
where the woodman's wife

dreams at night
of the stars that fall
to light the village parks.
And with the passing of time, and without mirrors in the room,
F. Al-Azzawi will have become even more aged than time itself
and his face will be an almanac of seasonal winds.
Q: What do people know about me?
A. Obscure and bare like an unfinished prophecy.
Q: Does the man made of stone flowers know which passions still linger
    in the eyes of the dead?
A: Fine, Fadhil Al-Azzawi wishes to unveil the sea once in his lifetime, to
drop his thousand birds in the jungle of new politics where the homeland
is a sign hung on the shoulders of shepherds, and where lovers forget to
edify to the custodians of fire.

Look:
all these construction bids for the reforestation of the heart
will not be enough to take a single man
to truth
as she sleeps in the gallows.

13

At last
I stood alone
on a mountain by a river
that turns twice around itself.
I looked at it
and I was sad for my sadness.
I cried, but my voice
disowned me.
It shattered in the wind while the wind that blows between me and life
    was singing.
I went down to the river (taking my wound along). I washed. And on
    the grass the day rolled past
like a chain circling a stone a thousand years wide.
It turned around itself and went toward the river and drowned its limbs.
It joined fire and water,
and joined me with the great pain.

14

Because the fruit of delusion tortures the eaters of reality,
because truth does not dare cross over to the king,
because cities in reality are more beautiful than in tourist brochures,
I watch chairs as they sit quietly
and talk about those who sit on them.
What world is this where fingers become
candy for birth certificates! and bomb-souvenirs
dangle from girls' chests!
What peace fills the country
and sits among lovers who lead truth to exile
while the continents are crowded and mankind remains our hope?

15

While cities were left to the wind,
I, who am deferred from the moment of birth,
bumped into reality and it shattered as its water broke
on a sidewalk.
I moved away from night and it moved closer to me.
It scratched its head before the police and the wounded.
No one smiled at me.
No one was there.
Open all the doors
for I love it when Salima looks toward God when she is with me.
"When are you with me, Salima?"
"When we do not exist, not even in poems."
There are boats. Look at the sea, and you will find a moon, waves, and
       stolen freedoms.
Cry out loud
and shepherds will slide from your lips.
Cry out in silence.

SONG OF THE DEAD ARAB

Left to the wind that dwells in the fields,
time and time again, you built the gardens of Babel.
Time and time again, you lifted stones to raise towers,
time and time again, you crossed rivers
and built your temples to the wind
where priests recited their old incantations.
Time and time again, you crossed the Empty Quarter
and created a civilization with the tip of your proverbial spear,
O beautiful Arab.
But as you die now, starving, your lips parted,
I'll call you Homeland, if you wish
and my name will be Life.
You are dying on the sidewalk of a street wet with dew,
and I look into your eyes and fail to recognize you.

THE MURDERED

From time to time the murdered one rises from his hole
and wipes the dirt off his forehead.
The road takes his feet
to the marketplace.
The people grab him:
"You've escaped once again!"
and they hang his old face
in another celebration.
The murdered one returns to his hole,
and the people go back to their business in the marketplace.

THE PEDESTRIAN

In the middle of the road to my life I lost my way: I strike the oar right and left. The lake is iron, and I hear myself forgetting the uproar of history. Ah, how difficult to describe this road that grinds me with fear and anxiety.

Is it the road to life seeping through my fingers like air? The road to my life more bitter than death. I should have gotten up and risen, but fear has entered me.

I walked on and saw villages scattered like sapphires on the hills. A transparent alley, sun-drenched, led me to a mountain of silver. Do I dare walk on? My spirit weakened and I turned around. A cry surprised me: "Let go of all fears from your soul and move on."

And I stepped alone toward freedom.

SOMETIMES WE ARE BORN

Sometimes we are born
and in our hands are the torturer's saw
or the woodman's axe
or the ember of the ruler's cigar
or
or . . .
Sometimes we are born, and in our mouths
the taste of death.

from *The Eastern Tree*

(1975)

THE OPENING

I know I am not a prince from Najd or a king from Babel.
I am not a prophet who walks on water
or makes in the smith's pyre the keys to the coffers of wisdom.
I know I am a man like the millions of the poor
writing my hunger . . .
I sit in the cold alone, the wind searing my face.
Sometimes the police strike me or jail me in a forgotten camp in the
          steppes of the Levant.
And if I love, they cut off my tongue so it would not speak its love.
Sometimes I am crammed among the deported
and I see myself a slave from Yathrib,
or a scoundrel roaming through Baghdad,
or an Egyptian soldier in Sinai suffering from the thirst of the six days,
or a man to be hanged, walking alone, challenging his torturers.
Sometimes I pick flowers
and give them to children.
Sometimes I harvest thorns.
Sometimes I laugh, sometimes I weep so that
my human heart would not rust.
I do nothing well except write poems
because I came to sing of mankind and to write its sadness.
If my song is heard like a weeping in a prison cell,
it is because I heard nothing except the howling of generations
carried by the wind.
And if my poems are poured on the sand,
it is because I dream the forgotten will read them
and that love will be my guide to the heart of man.

THE VALLEY OF THE BEASTS

As I went down into the valley of the beasts, I saw a fawn near a palm grove prancing. I saw birds chirping. I saw wolves crossing a plain and man was distant.

Then a call rose from within him. "Don't be sad, you are walking along the night of history. You will enter days lit with celebrations, and you will see days shut away in grief. Are you afraid of the dragon resting peacefully in his hiding place in the jungle, and forget that you are more of a killer?" Then the one emerging from the skin of death said, "I didn't kill anyone." And the voice said, "You will kill or will be killed. This is a time of killing." I cried, "But I came to learn, not to kill," and I walked on lonely within myself, poorer than a shrouded corpse in a coffin.

WRITE YOUR NAME ON EVERY PAIN

Shall I say, "History begins here,
and here the history of death dies?"
"Write, Abdullah, your history on a wave."
I said, "What shall I write?
     Shall I write about myself while I lick my wound?
     Shall I write about a country being murdered?
     Shall I write about a voice crying out in the wilderness?"
"Write your name on every pain,
     for the pangs of birth are cruel."

MAN IS NOTHING BUT A WOODSMAN IN THE FOREST

"Man is nothing but a woodsman in the forest,"
said the trees standing along the road.
And I too said, "What my soul needs is a woodsman."

"Man is nothing but a hunter,"
said a bird floating above the valley.
And I too said, "What my soul needs is a hunter."

"Man is nothing but a blind king,"
said the day shining above me.
And I too said, "What my soul needs is a blind king."

"Man is nothing but a torturer weeping,"
said a donkey grazing in the field.
And I too said, "What my soul needs is a torturer weeping."

"Man is nothing but a mound of sand and bones,"
said a wind beating my face.
Shivering, I carried his bones and let the wind scatter the sand.

ABDULLAH BEGS FROM THE SEA

And Abdullah saw the sea and told it,
"Travel has worn me out, and my soul longs to ride the waves,
but I have neither gold nor silver."
The sea said,
"Aren't you ashamed of begging from me?
I own myself
and that suffices me.
Go, Abdullah, and become a man who does not ask, but takes."
Abdullah felt ashamed
and threw his burdens into the sea.

THE KEY

"Don't be sad, Abdullah. Walk through the enchanted desert where the trees forever sing, and give your hand to the wind. On your shoulders birds will rest, and the Bedouins will come to you with garlands of desert flowers. They will weep at your door calling, 'We have been wrong,' and they will say to you, 'Tell us what to do or not to do, what to know or not know.' This is your land, Abdullah, and these are your people wailing on the roads, lonely and weighed by the immensity of the world. Would you not give a shirt to the naked, bread to the hungry, and love to the unloved? Would you not say 'Be!' so that you would become?"

Abdullah heard himself, his voice resounding in the wilderness,
"How can I be lonely when I have your love, my people?
How can I be a prisoner when I have the key to the future?"

THE LOVER

Do you remember the forest, Abdullah? How we went into it, the scent of the yellowed leaves under the trees filling us. Exhausted by love, we crossed green valleys and blue ones, and we saw a vixen run under grapevine, a bird fluttering between a stone and wild flowers. We sat under night's lanterns and recalled the happiness of the Kurdish women who spoke to us from the base of the snow-covered mountain the way princesses from a lost age laugh. The doves of the valley ran along our feet and you called to the prettiest among them, "Come, come closer to the strangers to the valley."
"What do you wish, master of the valley?"
"Nothing except that I am a lover."
"What can I do for the lover, O master of the valley?"
"Nothing except that I am a lover."
And she ran away after love made her blush, embarrassed.
"But who are you?"
She says, "Don't you know the answer, Abdullah?"
Then you woke up.
Do you remember, Abdullah, as we returned alone to the forest at dawn when the sound of the shepherd walking by a spring awakened us?

IN THE VILLAGE OF CHILDREN

And the traveler in the wilderness saw a drummer banging a drum, and people singing. Women were dancing and children sat on tree branches gazing at the scene with vacant eyes. I said to myself, "This is the wedding of man," and I entered the village thrilled by the fragrance of the grass and the scent of celebration.
The people saw me and came gladly toward me and said, "come on over, you are the king of strangers."
And I sat on a throne of ivory and I began to look at the people.
A man with a limp in his leg came toward me and said, "Do you know what the wound bleeding from the heart is like?"
"Whoever is wounded should not announce his wound," I said.
Then I saw a woman wailing before me.
"Tell us about the pain of death," she said.
I said, "And do I know the pain of birth?"
Then the children crowded before me and asked,
"Who are you looking for Abdullah?"
I said, "The absent man."
They said, "He may be the child sleeping under the tree."
"I don't know."
They said, "Leave our village, Abdullah,
and learn to see in the eyes of children
the man you seek."

A DONKEY AT A MILL

And my feet led me to a wheat mill at the low end of a village.
I saw a donkey gasping, exhausted in the heat. A miller was flogging
      him with a whip.
The miller said to me gruffly,
"I mill the wheat of the poor, what do you mill?"
I said, "I came to console the millers."
He was surprised by what I said.
"Well, sometimes man becomes lonely in a mill. Come here and take
      your turn."
The miller undid the bridle of the donkey and led him to the pasture.
I began to turn and the miller began whipping my back.
His donkey mumbled from a distance,
"Thank you, Abdullah."

AN APPOINTMENT IN SAMARRA

When I was in Baghdad, an old, pockmarked man prophesied my death
  to me.
I escaped to Samarra alone at night and thought, "Death does not
  know me here."
I entered my father's orchards, thronged with happiness and dreams
and spent my days composing poems.
Then times changed and I could no longer tolerate my solitude,
so I walked out to the street seeking solace among people.
The street was empty like death,
and I began to call out until the old, pockmarked man stopped me:
"What are you doing here in the house of the dead, Abdullah?"
I said, "This is the house of the dead?"
He said, "Here the wind combs the bats' hair."
I said, "What do I do?"
He said, "Get out of your death, Abdullah,
and learn how to raise your head like a palm tree
challenging the wind."
Let whoever dies rise. This is my voice crying out in the wilderness.

THE ROOM

He said, "Trees die if they don't shed their greenness.
Nothing here escapes his law.
The blind man sleeps on his violin,
the coachman returns at night from a bar,
and likewise this soldier sits by a river.
When the light of eternity falls into the soul,
a bird behind a fence trembles.
Other green branches begin to sway. We enter the room without candles."

IN PRISON

Faint screams slip through the keyhole. There were shadows of armed soldiers cast on an olivewood fence. At midnight a guard arrived. He called out some names: They were trembling with fear. He called out, "Come!"

The young man was thinking of his mother. "Where are my shoes," he asked the guard. "No shoes, hurry up!" and they left. The sounds of the night faded into silence at last.

Then we heard ten bullets ring out in the dark. I stood up in silence and put on his shoes in memoriam.

SIGNS

Look, there are clouds raining behind the forest.
Then the sun rises and the desert sand shoots up with grass.
Look, there is a wind howling between the trees.
Then birds come and doze after a long journey.
Look, there is a child playing happily among the waves
and they rise high and drown him in night.
Then the sailors sing his tale to ward off their sadness.

THE DRAGON'S MOUNTAIN

A blue mountain buried in night behind the forest—
three children run toward it. (This is the dragon's hut.)
"What do we do on the magic mountain?"
"We peek into his house and go back."
"No, I'll go back by myself."
The forest rained and the children sought refuge in the cave where
        Abdullah lived.
Terrified, the first child asked,
"Are you a friend of the dragon?"
The second child said,
"Let's go back."
The third child said,
"Leave us alone."
Abdullah sighed and said,
"Each of us has his dragon. This one is mine.
It's written that I must kill him so that I may live in the house of man."
The children, filled with excitement, went back to the village and told
        stories of Abdullah who lived on the dragon's mountain.

THE LIFE AND TIMES OF THE DRAGON

The dragon is sleeping on his stone.
He is dreaming of his children.
His teeth are dripping with blood.
It's from the wound he gave to the hunter.
His eyes are staring at the night sky.
He is stealing the light of the stars.
His growls can be heard for generations.
It's the death of his terrified victims.

The dragon
        is
                dying.

SO THAT WE DO NOT FORGET

"This is Abdullah who killed the dragon of the forest,"
said the man sitting at the village gate.
The people crowded around him singing, drunk with the happiness of
     freedom.
The king sat him beside him on his throne.
The commander gave Abdullah his sword,
and they built a statue of him in the village square.
But the man carrying the skin of the dragon
threw it over the statue and said:
"Whoever forgets the skin of the dragon
has never known me."

HAPPINESS

"They left me a window from which to see the trees,"
said the poet to himself as he walked to his cell.
They brought a carpenter and shut down the window.

"What happiness! It'll be enough to hear the wind shake the trees,"
        said the poet.
They brought a woodsman and he cut down the trees.

"The sound of the wind will suffice me,"
        said the poet.
They raised walls so the winds could not blow over them.

"It's enough that I am alive."

They raised a gallows in the yard.
The poet smiled,
"As I climb the ladder of my death,
I write my poems in the memory of the future."

EPILOGUE

And at last Abdullah saw light glimmering from the farthest ends of
      the future. He said,
"So there is man," and he walked further under sun and rain.
Then, "Oh how far is the house of man!" he said to himself.

He walked a long time and the light was still away.
"How short are the days of man searching for light!"
he told himself.
In the beginning he saw a man following him and said,
"What do you want from me?"
"I seek a kingdom glittering in the night."
"The road is long,
and the life of man is short."
"Oh how wretched is man who does know not his way!"

One day he turned around him and was startled
to see a crowd of phantoms.
"Who are you?"
"We seek a light like you."
He walked a long time, days, years, and the light was far away.
He saw people (farmers, workers, fishermen, children, and soldiers)
      running behind him.
He was amazed to see people running in a desert. They said,
"Don't be amazed, Abdullah, amazement is a delusion,
      and if man is deluded he dies."
Abdullah's soul darkened . . .
"Oh, how far I am from your light, kingdom of freedom," he thought,
and Abdullah walked months, other years, and ages,
and the light was still far away,
and behind him people were walking.

"Oh, how happy I am!" he said,
then Abdullah lay on the grass and died.

But the parade went on (farmers, workers, fishermen, children, and
    soldiers)
in the desert and across rivers to the light coming from the darkness of
    days.

If you see the parade, Abdullah, I mean you, reader of my poems,
on the street or in your house,
now or on all days,
follow it and do not ask where it is going.
Perhaps some day you will enter
the history of man.

from *A Man Throws Stones into a Well*

(1978–1988)

DEFIANCE

Eve came down from heaven followed by Adam.
They inhabited the earth, built soaring towers, cities of stone in the
        wilderness, and on the sea ships made of metal.
They created a people that became races that created nations.

They used to overstuff themselves
and sometimes a deadly hunger ravished them,
and with the days they engaged in war
seeking a bloody glory
expounded upon by philosophers
and sung by poets.

Where is the first mother biting her apple, refusing to obey even God?
I will kiss her on the lips and tell her,
"Thank you, woman,
      first rebel,
      creator of freedom."

THE ROPE

Joseph was a boy from Babel.
His brothers threw him into a well,
but he, who was a magician,
always carried a rope with him,
a rope he will use to climb out with.
He knew that the wolf that ate him
will turn around
and return again
to the wilderness.

BROTHERHOOD

The wolf that ate Joseph in the wilderness
stared for a long time at the opening of the well.
He waited for that ancient child
who sat in the bottom alone
listening to the storms in his heart.
But Joseph who was to become king
of a dead Jerusalem,
placed his hand on the wolf and blessed him
and the two walked out into history
leaving their traces
on the sand
like a password whispered at night.

COCKROACH

One morning, like all living creatures, Gregor Samsa woke up
and was surprised to find that he had become a cockroach.
So he thought of avenging himself
by going up to Kafka's room at night
to eat up his novels in the castle.

Don't be angry, household cockroach, Gregor Samsa.
There's still a bed you can hide under
and nooks for you to live in
and crumbs you can steal at night from the kitchen.
And finally, what's the use?
You are after all Gregor Samsa.

THE THREE KINGS

The first king opened his eyes and stared at a star
glimmering, a pearl at night.
The second king lay on the grass and thought of
a child being born out of a wound.
As for the third king, who was coming from the end of the world
to witness the birth of God,
he saw the star in the valley go out and the night begin:
Another antichrist is at the gates Sodom.

Ah, how unbearable this journey has been!
How unbearable this false prophecy!

THE LAST IRAQ

Each night I sit Iraq on my table
and pinch his ears
until his eyes fill up with tears
of joy.
Another cold winter, crisscrossed by jet fighters.
Soldiers sit on a hillside
waiting for history
to rise from the darkness of Ahwar,
a rifle in its hand
shooting out angels
training for the revolution.
Each night I place my hand on Iraq,
and he slips through my fingers
like soldiers fleeing the front.

MEMORY

Memory stands
before a shore crowded with shells,
then sits on a swing
and sways into a hospital whose patients are
she-elephants,
child serpents,
stone squirrels,
and princess-trees
carrying a forgotten wave on their shoulders.

Memory sits
in her sand cave
and issues its first communiqué
against me.

from *At the End of All Journeys*

(1994)

IN THE COURT OF HONOR

In one of my incomplete poems
a sentence challenged another
and slapped it with its glove
inviting it to a duel
in the Court of Honor.

At the end of the fight,
and as happens often,
one of my sentences was dead
and the other bleeding on the page.
I did not want to get involved
in the maze of criminal investigations
between questions and answers.
I decided to wash my hands
of their blood,
and threw away the whole poem.

VISION ON A BUS

As I was traveling by bus
between this life and the hereafter
the angel Gabriel hopped in
(a hat on his head, its rim
bent over his forehead)
wearing a long coat
and looking like one of the fugitives
on the sidewalks of Bahnhof Zoo.
He got in without buying a ticket
and sat on the seat beside me
pretending to look through the window
like an American tourist.
As we drove on, he poked my side
and began reciting his new holy verses
into a tape recorder he held in his hand.
His monotonous voice nauseated me
and I got up to escape.
But he caught up with me
and threw me back into my seat.
He pressed his pistol against my chest
and said threatening, "Next time,
O prophet, I shall shoot.
Now recite! Recite
in the name of thine Lord who created thee!"

A MAN IN MEMORY

For many years
he kept panting behind me
like a deranged dog,
from protest to protest,
from trial to trial,
from alley to alley,
café to café.
In the morning, on my way to college,
I used to see him standing in front of the black gate,
smoking and leaning on his bicycle.
And at noon, heading to the student club,
I noticed him sitting on the dirt platform
of the northbound train,
holding an egg sandwich, devouring it,
and looking for me with his deep-set eyes.
He knew no one except me
and so he recorded my name
in every report he gave to the police
in Aiwadiya.
After many years
(and I had forgotten him by then)
they took me in once
to stand before a military court
whose members were suffering from boredom,
and who had pulled out some ragged papers—
paper that mice had been feeding on—
in order to pass the time.
They brought him to witness against me
as he had always done.
But as soon as he saw me surrounded by soldiers in the hall,
he hurried toward me and greeted me like a lost brother.
They had thrown him out on the street
after he'd gotten old and was out of strength.
He told me, "No one needs me and I have always served them."
When they called his name, he entered the courtroom stumbling, drunk.

He must have downed a bottle of arak beforehand.
He put his hand on the Quran
and swore that I was the noblest man he'd ever met in his life
and that all he'd said about me in the past
was a lie and outright slander.
So the court forgave me
the many transgressions I did not commit
and declared me a good citizen
in the annals of the state.

On the way to the city
we rode the same bus and he sat beside me
and asked me shyly
to reward him with a bottle of arak.
I bought him a whole box
and he carried it and left.
After two or three months
he came to my office drunk.
He dropped his head and began to cry
and talked about his young wife
who was cheating on him
with secret friends
whenever he went to the bar at night.

Every two or three months
he came to me
to give him enough money to keep him drunk for a week,
then he'd leave tripping on his own steps.
Months passed and he did not come again
and I thought he'd died at last.
But then he showed up one last time
and sat in a chair in front of my desk
and apologized for his whole life.
Completely sober, he said,
"Give me two dinars and you won't see me after today.
I will disappear from your life forever."
When he got up he shook my hand warmly (which was unlike him)
as if he were a friend leaving for a distant city.

After a few days I learned that he'd slit his own throat with a razor.

SONG OF MYSELF

When I reached ten
I said to myself:
Everything will be all right, Fadhil,
as long as there are seasons turning,
as long as winter surprises you with its rain
and spring with its wild flowers
and summer with its blazing August
and autumn with its profound sadness,
as long as you sit on the front step of your family home in Kirkuk
watching black clouds in a red sky, fleeing,
followed by horses and elephants.
I said: When you get to be twenty,
you'll go to Musallah garden
and stroll the afternoon at the foot of Said Gezi hill,
and in the evening you'll sit at a café near Qaisaria
and stare at the small storks,
perched on top of Naqishli Manara Si tower,
while they chirp for you.

When I turned twenty
I wasn't in a park or a café,
but in Baghdad Prison
guarded by policemen from the country who woke us up every morning
to run ahead of their clubs with which they beat us,
forcing us to squat in "the grid"
of long lines
and be counted like sheep inspected by the butcher
before the slaughterhouse.
I said then: Everything will be all right, Fadhil,
as long as all of life is still ahead of you
and your heart is filled with hope.
When you're thirty
you'll return to your family,
and your missing friends will come to you
from their new places of refuge

to tell you about cities on the Tropic of Capricorn
and others on the Pole.

And when I reached thirty
I myself was in exile.
I said: Everything will be all right, Fadhil.
When you're forty
you'll go back to your penniless poet friends
who will wait for you in the evening
sitting on benches on the sidewalk
sipping tea from Café Majid.
You'll get drunk together night after night
at the Aadliya Club
cussing out the government
and loafing about on the empty streets
until dawn.

And when I reached forty
I saw them all escaping, one after another,
with fake passports,
or crossing borders
with smugglers leading donkeys
through dangerous mountainous terrains.
And we got drunk together
once here and once there
in Berlin or Cyprus,
or London or Paris,
and sometimes
in hell.
I said: Everything will be all right, Fadhil,
as long as your memories are with you, at least.
When you turn fifty
you'll go back to your forgotten tree
to water it from your palms,
rebuild your house
which the termites have eaten,
and retrieve your books, left behind in cardboard boxes,
and read them again.

And when I turned fifty
I saw our old tree cut down with an axe,
our house infested with rats,
and my books thrown into the well.

And now what will you say to yourself, Fadhil,
now that you've burned all the ships you left behind?
Oh, I don't want to say anything,
I won't say a thing.
Leave me alone, damn it!
I've reached the end in one second
and learned all the wisdom of the world even before realizing
what had happened.

GOOD MORNING, GOD

Good morning, God!
I'm sure you know me well,
even though we've never met,
for you know all by name,
one by one,
the good ones and the bad.
I really wanted to visit you
to offer my loyal obedience,
but I didn't know your address in the sky
where there is a maze of stars and galaxies.
You know I'm not an astronaut
and I don't have a vehicle to carry me to you.
I know you're very busy.
In truth, we're all busy these days
even though I've been unemployed forever.
Still, I ask you to please listen to me
as I tell you my views on everything.
After all, you created me and threw me all alone
on this wretched planet.
I heard so much about you
even before I was born.
They talk about you respectfully
but with bad intentions.
I believe they intend to harm you, sir.
They're all afraid of being shipped to hell
in closed cars,
or are greedy for furnished apartments in heaven.
You know this better than I do, I'm sure.
That must be annoying, isn't it?
But why should I care about this
since I only wanted to talk to you as a friend
who's not concerned about gains or losses
and since I wanted to talk to you
heart to heart
as they say?

I thought of calling you,
but I couldn't find your name
in the phone book,
and so it'll make me very happy
if you'd call me
and try to lift my spirits,
asking me jokingly,
"How are you doing, Fadhil,
in this ephemeral world?"
You know my phone number.
Call me any time you like,
night or day.
I spend most of my time at home
reading or writing or watching television,
and sometimes I doze off while
thinking about the future of the world.
Really, let's get together, even once.
You too need a break.
There's a lot I want to tell you,
a lot I haven't told anyone,
a lot I can't tell anyone but you.
And if you like, I'll read you my latest poems
so that you'll tell me what you think honestly.
Maybe we'll talk about the fate of humanity
or the fate of the universe
over a cup of coffee.
I have many plans and ideas.
I think you'll like them.
I'd prefer we meet at my place,
and, at any rate, you know the address.
My name is written on the door.
Just ring the bell once
and you'll hear me call from inside,
"The door is open. Welcome, God. Step in.
I've been waiting for you forever."

THE PRODIGAL SON RETURNS

I got to walk that lonesome valley
I got to walk it all by myself
No one can walk it for me
I got to walk it all by myself
　　　　　　　—"Lonesome Valley," a gospel song

1)　　I open my eyes and see the sun through the curtain.
The rooster has returned to its coop
after it crowed three times from a wall
at the break of dawn.
The morning opens up over the roof
and goes down the stairway, step by step.
Even the lone tree in the courtyard
is filled with anxious birds
landing in waves
from a blue sky open
like an overturned abyss.

There I heard the blind reciter,
whose son was dragged into the army,
recite verses of the Quran
I learned by heart:
　　　　Alam tara kaifa faala rubbaka bi-Aad.
　　　　Irama thatal-imad
　　　　al-lati lam yukhlaq mithluha fil-bilad
　　　　wa Thamud al-dheen jabul skhara bil-wad
　　　　wa Firawana thil awtad.
Rising from sleep, I lift my head
like a child dreaming of heaven
surprised I'm still alive.
All this light from the past!
All this noise in the city!
I open my eyes, and fingers of light close them.
I think of a coachman whipping his two ragged horses
there in the dusty alley
where a cart stops in front of our house

and an old man gets out, his hands creased,
his eyes two cold holes,
returning from his distant exile
after a thousand years spent in strange cities
begging ghosts for love
and his memories for repose.
On the stone stairway
I meet him
carrying the suitcase he bought
from a Jewish shop in Frankfurt.
Then he takes off his black sunglasses
and whisks me in his arms
taking me to wash my face near the well, mumbling:
> *Wohin des Wegs? Du stehst am Ufer Hier.*
> *Ich bin bereit, dich durch den Fluss zu tragen.*
Look, the cactus fruit has grown in the garden.
The sunflower plant is tall again.
He lay there tossing his memories before me on the sand,
weeping over the child he once was.
> *To see the World in a Grain of Sand*
> *And Heaven in a Wild Flower*
> *Hold Infinity in the palm of your hand*
> *And Eternity in an Hour.*
Ah, tell me who guided you to the valley of ghosts?
What call led you to this fate?
Nothing except that I rose and saw the forest.
Nothing except that I saw a swarm of angels at dawn
going down into the valley, into the set traps.
We caught many of them
and that was all.
Believe me.

2)   What have you won from your betting, gambler?—
standing by the ocean setting asail your paper boats,
waiting to arrive on another continent
to build a kingdom where the devil had been chased out
with sticks and brooms.
He flees to heaven and leaves his victims behind
to chew on their memories.

What have you gained from your madness, O mad one?—
gripping your staff,
roving from one village to another,
from season to season
passing fires lit at night
by beggars who carry
bags filled with snakes.

What have you gained from your defiance, O rebel?—
refusing to eat from the meat of sacrifices,
spilling your holy wine
in the gods' feasts,
tossing pearls under people's feet,
hammering with your shivering hand
a poisoned nail
into your own heart.

What have you gained, O poet, from your wandering?

3)   In broken mirrors a face steals a glimpse
of an age that has yet to come;
its arches hang in the air while the screaming soul of the prairie
wanders, in tears, wearing her only mourning dress,
holding my hand and gnawing at me with vampire teeth.
Never turn around.
Don't turn to the swallow left on the tree.
The charcoal sky nears our faces
like a dream that lives in the head, a dream a hunter plucks with a
        knife
and offers as bait to kindhearted whores
who walk at night on half-drunk streets
followed by children wearing pirates' clothes.
In every corner there is a mirror.
Once I saw murderers standing at alley crossings
leaning on their rifles, sipping tea.
Finally the evicted workers came out
of their caves, following a bus crowded with thieves.
This is not the right place for regretting mistakes.

There under the tree we can sit and deliberate
the future of the world.
Have you ever seen a plane bomb a demonstration?
You can comfortably say I was there
when the sky rained bombs.
I saw the pilot staring at us from his window.
I cursed him, but he ignored me.
His face remained stuck in my mirror
which I threw underfoot. The crowds stomped upon it
and it caught corpses from burned tanks
decorated with flags and posters.
In memory, there is always a portrait of a quarrelsome devil
sticking his tongue out at me,
sitting at his exquisite desk
under searchlights.

4)   Which markets have you walked? How many women have you
met wrapped in black robes crossing Old Qaisariya to your house followed
by a young Kurdish porter, his pushcart filled with pomegranates and
oranges? How many times have you climbed the fort? How many times
have you come down from the fort on the way to the cinema to watch a
film about Tarzan among the apes of the jungle on your way to the café to
meet friends who sit in the evening and drink tea, talking about Gorky's
mother or Hemingway's fish? How many times have you crossed Khassat
Su river, skipping stones to reach a retreat on the other side of the city and
avoiding the spies on their bicycles? How many times have you combed
your hair and oiled it? How many times have you parted it hoping she'd see
you, the Turkoman girl you loved?
What cities have you left? What villages?
How many friends left you without saying goodbye?
How many wars broke out in which you were not killed?
How many jails have you been thrown in?
How many poems have you written?
How many times have you walked down al-Rashid Street
and found yourself in a village on the German border?
And the trial they held for you in Basra,
how did it turn into a café in Leipzig?
And the fat torturer in Al-Hilla Prison,

why did he twine his thick moustache
while carrying his ropes on his shoulder?
And the clowns, why did they lead their monkeys
from the cane huts to the stone barracks?
And the grave diggers, how did they load their coffins
on carts pulled by donkeys,
and slide from the orphaned hill
to the spring
to wash their hands from blood and dust before riding on again.

5)   Each act of volition is a sign of fire.
Each fire is a sign of ash.
Each grain of ash is a sign of stone with which the future is built.
Each future is a sign of whatever rises now.
And what rises now is a sign of a cry that goes unheard.
Each unheard cry is a sign of the one you cried before.

What belongs to Caesar will be yours alone.
The mountain will come willingly to talk to you.
Ah, don't tell him anything,
for you must have secrets of your own.
Tell him you've waited too long
and he'll understand.
This planet is the first stop
on your way home.

NO MATTER HOW FAR

Whenever a hand leans on the fence, the one ruined by soldiers coming from villages and distant cities on their way to their barracks, a slave stands by the castle's curtain and blows into a horn. A hawk spreads his wings and swoops down toward my heart, which I had left in the prairie, beasts licking its blood as they groveled out of their dens.

Here between cities suspended in memory like lanterns at night, between dirt roads at noon trodden by tired caravans heading for a cave where thieves hid their treasures, I walk, the wind behind my shoulders, knowing that a man will meet me at the end of the journey or its beginning, and that I'll be his guest whom I will kill one night and escape, leaving footsteps on the sand.

All these kingdoms, how do I enter them? All these stretched hands, how can I refuse them? All these wars, how can I lose them? All these rituals, how can I desecrate them?

Ah, nothing except this arm that cannot reach out, this severed arm behind a fence where dried grasses are piled in the sun, and nothing except a pair of eyes watching soldiers with bayoneted rifles stabbing the wounded behind the trees.

And there on a grassy hill inhabited by birds and jackals I see astronauts landing their spaceships and leaving their gifts on the open road.

From behind the fence surrounding heaven, I watch God with his roughened hands vexedly kneading Adam's clay, leaving it in the sun to dry. I distract him and it is I who blows life into the statue. Adam rises to greet me with an embrace, "You are my son. I've been waiting for you." Fleeing, we climb mountains leaving God in his solitude making new statues.

There isn't a single star out tonight. The longer we wait, the longer its absence extends. The moon in its waning and the wolf in the cave.

Poisoned algae on the soul, and a coachman whips his horse in the morning. At the foot of the hill grasshoppers bounce about, and plastic devils studded with rubies and jasper stroll public parks. There, finally, from the first caves, the ape tribes come out, and we join them happily and descend toward the spring.

No matter how far
my horse takes me,
in the end there is always
a cheap hotel awaiting us
and a stable full of hay.

GOD AND THE DEVIL

In the first chapter we talk
about a devil who defies God.
In the second chapter
about expelling Satan from Paradise.
In the third chapter
about Adam's dilemma.
In the fourth
about the deluge.

Then finally someone comes along
and snatches Satan
and the good God masters the whole world.

What are we going to talk about
in the fifth chapter
and the sixth
and the seventh
and the eighth, etc.?

ELEGY FOR THE LIVING
(Iraq: January 17, 1991)

When I saw the parade
of soldiers up close
I felt a pang of pain:
how insipid they looked
marching past
              —Ishikawa Takabuk (1885–1912)

1

When the moon is full,
the murderers are out on the streets
holding their pocket knives
waiting for girls
at alley crossings.

When the moon is full,
Dracula rises
from his grave
and files his teeth with a sharpener
then drifts in his black cape toward the hunt.

When the moon is full,
the torturers shut their gates
and release wolves
into the city.

This is the hour when dragons
trudge out of their caves.
This is the hour of Adam,
the angels kicking the back of his neck,
dragging him out of Paradise.
This is the hour of Cane stabbing Abel with a knife.
This is the hour of Noah and the deluge has come.
This is the hour of Muhammad hiding in a cave
        comforting his companion in terror.

This is the hour of Hallaj crucified on his tree in Karkh.
This is the hour of Hulago on his white horse crossing a Tigris of blood.
This is the hour of the murderers.
This is the hour of the murdered.

A wave of planes followed by another wave,
eyes shine in the dark.
Guns quake above the towers
where flaming birds strike at space with their wings
then incinerate over the city.
Death in the sky and death on Earth.
Death in the fields and death in the desert.
Death in the body and death in the soul.
Death in the past and death in the future.
Death in life and death in death.
When the moon is full,
I see a white missile soaring above
branded with a dedication by a soldier from Boston
who wrote his message in blood:
To Mr. Hammurabi in BABYLON,
with love.
When the moon is full
all the enemies crawl from history
to hold their pagan rite.

2

You bombs named after the mistresses of soldiers from a dilapidated
continent, explode over Al-Rashid Street. Wipe out our memories, rip
over Al-Zahawi Café, over Hassan Ajami's coffee shop, over the Brazilian
Café, over Café Samar, and disintegrate on Abu Nawas Beach where the
fish of the Tigris have fled never to return.

Blood on the asphalt, blood on Al-Mutanabbi's face as he recites his poems
in Tahrir Square. Blood on the forehead of Abu Aala Al-Maari, the blind
poet, as he paces back and forth between Rasafah and Karkh, walking the
alleyways, making his way with his staff through ruins left behind by cruise
missiles and cluster bombs. He asks the passers-by, "I believe I've reached

the Day of Doom. Is it so?" And the voice of a wailing woman answers, "No, poet, it is war. They kill so that righteousness overtakes the hearts." And he grumbles:

> In every age there are fallacies
> > firmly held within.
> But has any generation marked itself
> > with truth as doctrine?

Blood on Ashurbanipal's golden carriage, on Gilgamesh's face as he searches for immortality. Blood on Maruf Al-Rasafi's kaffiyeh, blood on Al-Jawahiri's hat. Blood on Jawad Salim's statue after his horse flees for its life. Blood on Abdulqader Al-Gailani in his mosque. Blood on the unknown soldier who is no longer unknown, on the hair of the girls we loved and the ones we could have loved tomorrow.

You bombs, you poisoned gifts, I send you back to America, without spite or hatred. I return you to Walt Whitman, to Robert Frost, to William Faulkner, to William Carlos Williams, to Henry Miller, to Anaïs Nin, to Allen Ginsberg, to Ferlinghetti, to the Blacks in Harlem, to the men of the Federal Bureau of Investigation, to the retired murderers returning from Vietnam, to the industrious spies and their radar ears that probe the sky, to Marilyn Monroe whom we miss on nights of loneliness, to Elvis Presley teaching our dead to dance to rock 'n' roll, to Hemingway who will never be able to write after this war, to the slaves in their cages, ships from Africa taking them to plantations in the South, to Christopher Columbus who should have never discovered America. I send you back to your Statue of Liberty.

You bombs, looking like wild birds, I send you back to each city, street, and home in America. I send you to your children in their playgrounds, to the homeless on your streets, to the CEO's in their elegant offices, to the young prostitutes in the hotels where rooms are rented by the hour, to the generations of crack, to the UN building in New York, to the gurus of the American way, to private investigators in Chicago, to road robbers in Arizona, to the cowboys who made us laugh, to all those we loved and those we hated.

America,
I send you back your bombs
in boxes wrapped in gift paper
with my signature on them.
I send you back
the severed hands of Iraqi children,
and the corpses of soldiers buried in the sand,
and the black eyes of girls who have just come back
from a picnic.
America take your bombs,
and do whatever you want with your smart missiles.
Hunt whales with them,
or blow them up in your rear end if you wish,
in front of your television cameras
where capitalism sits
in her old carriage
greeting the crowds lining the streets
on her way to hell.

3

Here are the dead child soldiers sitting in Paradise (as the military declarations state) under olive and fig trees, before rivers of honey and streams of milk, embracing (though they never tasted women in their lives) blond nymphs, not even wearing bikinis, lying on heaven's grass.

Death, come and take us on a stretcher
and raise us to eternity.

A world spitting blood, where there is no history except the history of the murderer. Jet fighters soar above a hospital. Missiles pass over the heads of shepherds who leave their flocks to poisoned springs.

On this night, and on every night, I hear the cries of the children of Iraq under ruins. I hear my mother lamenting her sons going to war. I hear the despair of the voiceless and the pride of the dead. I hear a new Iraq being born with every spilled drop of blood.

In the distance I see airplanes coming, flown by Bedouin dictators, their shoulders studded with stars, piercing the clouds, frightening birds in their skies. Below them the valleys stretch, crowded with caravans of captives beating their drums, heading toward another desert. And on the towers gun openings shine like eyes in a cave. Cities burn, boneless cities like snakes buried in mud. Jet fighters exchange kisses over the Tigris, blowing away its bridges, one after the other. And on the roof of Abu Nawas's apartment I stand and look at Baghdad, convulsing under my feet, swallowing its destruction.

Here I am in Kirkuk, as the airplanes return from battle, as smoke rises from burned houses.

I search for armless children, for Khassat Su River, for Al-Alamain Garden, for Majidiya Café, for the murdered Kalaa.

I search for my mother, walking over the rubble, her hands stained with the blood of her sons.

Abandoned streets, nothing except ghosts. Nothing except a dragon roaming in his tank. And in Baba Karkar, I see the corpses of the workers, on the eternal fields of fire.

4

On this night
as bloods washes my face,
I sit in my shelter staring silently
at the decrepit sky
torn by planes coming from the Day of Doom,
at Baghdad whose mouth they have filled with zaqqum,
at the burned houses,
at the streets where minotaurs roam wailing to no end
among crowds fleeing from hell to hell,
at a spider, its eyes glittering in the dark,
awaiting its prey,
at Miss Liberty abandoning her platform in New York,
tearing her clothes off in an empty square

offering herself to the dogs,
at the torturers as they emerge from history
crossing the Tigris in boats,
at a dawn crawling like an orphan at play
riding through the gardens of Ashurbanipal,
at a cart filled with corpses
pulled by panicked men
heading to God who is crucified at their doors.
On this night
hordes of murderers creep out of their hovels
into salty winds
robbing one city after another.

5

This is your night, Iraq:
a black winter, clouds howling in a desert,
and screams from huts of mud and lime.
No one on the streets except the ghost of war
staggering down the road.
No drunks returning home at the end of the night.
No taverns switching off their last lanterns.
Nothing except your old darkness,
and planes coming from every continent
to murder children who have just fallen asleep,
to murder men who have just come out of prison,
and mothers pondering their distant children
planting their trees in exile.

6

On this night,
I see death taking a stroll
and tossing his coins on the roads.

7

This is your night, Baghdad:
Dogs bark through the streets,
and trees burn in the wind.
Your blind guard
has rolled a chain around your throat
and led you with his whips
to torturers who blow fire
at your face.
Baghdad, they have sentenced you to death,
like a curse, eternal, an irreversible decree,
a plague moving from house to house,
from street to street.

8

This is your night, Iraq:
Mothers stand at the crossings of battle-bound roads,
waiting for their sons who will never return,
young soldiers who never grew up,
whose life is only the time of their death,
left in the desert
for the wolves to mangle.

9

On this night, and every night,
angels leave their thrones
above the sky
and descend to the streets after each raid.
They take down the names of the living
for their daily report to God.

10

Bedouins crouch on the sand,
sniffing the scent of corpses in the distance.
Friendly dictators
shake the hands of their statues in the squares.

11

This crucified one,
we will carry him
on our shoulders forever.

12

In murdered Iraq,
all power to the victims.

from *A Moth on Its Way to Fire*

(1998)

A MOVIE IN A TRAIN STATION

In a train station in winter, returning from a long journey,
I found myself in a movie theater for travelers
and watched a film with an unfamiliar plot.
It started before I got here,
a movie that never ends.
It does not matter when you start watching it.
Its scenes repeat
the way life's events recur.

Heroes don thieves' masks.
Armies crawl through snow to reach a city.
Clowns walk in front of carts dragged by tired horses.
Men wearing wings made of wax swim in space.
Insects take to their strange paths toward planets
under burning suns.
Someone finds a pearl and loses it again.
And we bleed on the sheets
of travelers' beds in a cheap, one-night hotel.

Dead spectators, living spectators.
Someone enters, another leaves.
The hall is always dark.
Our movie goes on without end.

FROM AN OPEN WINDOW
UNTO A DARK STREET

As I stare through my window
and listen to the conquerors' noises on the street
drawing their carts in the dark
followed by boys beating drums
and slaves and captives in chains,
ghosts come to knock on my door:
the torturer and his victim,
the king and his clown,
and the secretary.

The torturer comes to wash his bloody hands
under my faucet.
The victim offers me a cup of her salty tears.
The king installs his throne in my garden.
The clown performs his tricks for me.
And the secretary divulges all he knows.

I light the last of my candles
and stand before the window.
Many will knock on my door
before morning arrives.

TOASTS

Even though I am drunk and sad and can barely talk,
please allow me to propose another toast:
A toast to the blind who see in the dark
A toast to the mute who talk to God on the mountain
A toast to the deaf who listen to the music of eternity
A toast to the poet who steals fire from the gods
A toast to God to create a better world the next time around
A toast to Satan losing his bet and returning to hell
A toast to the mother under whose feet paradise lay
A toast to the beloved waiting on the shore
A toast to the friend who does not abandon us
       even when the rooster crows thrice
A toast to the deceiver who does not whisper evil in people's hearts
A toast to the noose that bends to the hanged man's neck
A toast to the torturer who flogs himself
A toast to the victim who rises from his torment
A toast to the bird that leaves the cage
A toast to exile that does not defeat our will
A toast to the homeland with rivers running beneath
A toast to freedom until the end
A toast to a world for all in collectivity
A toast to the despots we hire as museum guards
A toast to the tree with roots deep in the earth
A toast to the moon listening to lovers' laments
A toast to the sun in the bitter cold of February
A toast to the planets still rumbling about since the Big Bang
A toast to heaven on earth
A toast to hell pouring concrete over her closed gates
A toast to the past as it tells us its memories
A toast to the present gushing like a river in the streets
A toast to a future we climb without ladders
A toast to this beautiful, short life.

NOTHING HAPPENS IN MY DREAMS ANYMORE

No roc perched on her eggs,
or spreading her wings over the valley.
No spiraling archipelago
abandoned by pirates
heading toward another island.
No volcanoes erupting into the sea
and no earthquakes striking the earth.

Nothing happens in my dreams anymore.
No dragons emerge from the water in the fog
with mermaids snatched between their jaws.
No women committing suicide after failed loves.
No mad poets
falling on their faces at night in the roads.

Nothing ever happens in my dreams.
No wars breaking out.
No parades marching on festival days.
No ships arrive,
and no robots leading repentant dervishes to Paradise.

Nothing ever happens in my dreams.
The street is empty as usual
and I have to get home
before the rain comes pouring down.

THE BOOK OF LIES

After half an hour of flying
from Larnaca to Berlin,
the pretty hostess announced on the PA system
that one of the plane's engines has quit,
and fearing that we'll drop into the sea,
and seeking safety,
we'll return to our departure city.
Otherwise everything is fine.
I looked at the clouds piled outside the window.
Terrified, I thought it's not fair for me to die this way
on such a magical day.

The plane began to shake like an old truck
falling suddenly into a bottomless well,
while the sea with its whales and dancing dolphins
spread its blue carpet below us.

I must have been about die of terror
when my American neighbor
said confidently, "Don't be afraid.
All of this is just rubbish.
The plane won't crash just because its engine stopped."
Then he began to tell me horrific stories he'd lived through:
a plane whose captain died of a heart attack
above Africa's green jungles,
another whose engine swallowed a ton of birds
above Nevada's arid mountains,
and a third whose wings the wind tore off
in a sky above an ocean teeming with sharks.
But he always survived,
because airplanes
are the safest means of transportation in the world.

When the plane finally landed and surged to the gate,
and we at last breathed a sigh of relief,

my American neighbor pulled from his bag
a book that he gave me.
He shook my hand goodbye and said,
"Don't forget to read it. It's my latest work,
The Book of Lies."

NIGHT SOLDIERS

"May a battalion of German soldiers rape your mother!"
that's how adults cursed
in my small distant city
forty years ago.

Staring at the distant horizon,
I used to crouch in pain for the whole of my wasted day—
the sad mother
being ravished by thousands of soldiers returning
from the battle of Stalingrad
with their torn boots and tattered coats.

No one was there to tell me the truth,
so I stayed up every night
seeing thousands of dead soldiers walk down our dark street
dragging their rusty cannons behind them
and mumbling in Arabic with a heavy Saxon accent.

I went out to them,
my heart filled with horror,
holding our oil lamp
and offering them the cigarettes my father left on the table
so that they'd leave our city in peace.
But they always turned their faces away
and walked on disappearing into the dark.

THE RUSSIAN ELEGY

Because the prophet from Siberia has not arrived
they planted the corpses of the czars in Red Square.
Lenin usually stands in the balcony
stroking his pointed beard
like a brush in the hand of a painter who was just birthed by a dream.
He'd arrived on his German train protected from the excess of workers'
        pains
to greet the parades of the armed shoeless in St. Petersburg
emerging out of bears' hovels
to whip the back of time with their songs
which the slaves of the future will forget
as wasted screams on history's dining table.
Millions of heads were cut off:
Dostoyevsky gambled the last copeck in his pocket
while drinking wine in the cellar of his Prince Myshkin.
Pushkin fell smeared with his own blood
in his last bout with the devil,
and Tolstoy slipped out of Stalin's hand
and fled to his serfs.

I know that the most beautiful stones are those the flood carried away.
The most beautiful of the just are those we've never known.
The most beautiful trees are the ones that were pulled out by
        bulldozers.
The most beautiful children are the ones whose screams we never hear
        echoing out of prison cells.
The most beautiful poems are those written in boredom.

Russia, Russia,
it's all over now.
Take the funeral of your dead dreamer to your cold house.
Light a small candle for him in the church of your failed revolutions
and bury him secretly
in the freezing cold of your long bloody history.
Leave us our eternal dream of climbing the highest mountains—

our rainbow with which we'll illuminate the valleys of the future—
as the last and most difficult task in our lives,
and as we await the prophet for whom we still long
despite all the losses.

ON THE GRIFFON FARM

O great priest, great priest up high,
I saw you sneak into this poem while I was not paying attention,
to where a thousand griffons
grazed on a farm that stretches between the seasons,
fenced by electric wire.

I saw you fill your cages with them,
taking them to the street, letting them out to stroll the sidewalks,
chirping behind you until
the last scene in the age of the dead.
I saw you release them into insipid history
and toss them into the fire.

O priest, priest up high,
in your inferno I saw a storm spewing rats.
In the ash I saw torturers brandishing their hands.
In landfills I saw frogs search for swamps,
and at night I saw wolves howling away.

O priest, priest up high,
leave our griffons in peace
and get out of this poem.

THE MAGI IN OUR HOUSE

Misguiding the thieves
creeping about at night,
we hide the Holy Spirit,
with its gouged eyes,
in the refrigerator.

On the wall we hang seismographic charts
and chatter about Einstein and his black holes.
We sit in the kitchen and smoke.
Heavy water mixed with peppermint
boils in the kettle
while the blind goose that lays
the golden egg
roasts in the oven.

The Magi have come at last.
Salima says, "I'll make
an angel's breakfast
for our guests."
We change places and go
to the living room
and wait for our coffee.

Life has become really expensive:
all these hypotheses only to measure
the light curve,
all these victims to win a single war,
all these pharaohs only to ask
for a mummy's hand.
Nobody talks about all that now.
Nobody cares for others
because there is no proof of anything.
What is positive is also negative
like every hope, like every doubt.

Oh, so many mysterious tribes are wandering
among these empty galaxies.

In a garden, in a distant garden
we lie back under alien stars
and remind ourselves of our happy days
in Paradise.

THE IF POEM

O God,
if you'd created man with one hand
and three legs
what would the apes have said?
If you'd pinned long tails to our behinds,
how would we have danced at parties?
If you gave us wings to fly with,
what would we do with our passports?
If you'd made us invisible,
on whom will the spies write their reports?
If you'd given us nine fingers,
how would we count to ten?
If you'd made our bodies out of steel,
how would we fight our wars?
If you'd made our noses beaks,
how would we kiss the girls?
If you would govern us,
what would we do with our rulers?
If I give you this poem
what will you add to it?
If . . .
If . . .
If . . .
O God!

∞∞

THE WIDOW ON HER BALCONY

Wearing mourning attire,
my neighbor, the widow in the building opposite,
leans on the railing of her balcony
and smokes like me, waiting and worried,
one cigarette after another,
releasing her kisses into the air
to her dead husband
who's stepping out of the bus that has just arrived.

Her hot kisses
land on my lips.

ABRAHAM IN THE GARDEN OF FIRE

The temple guards were drunk, the priests fast asleep. The primary god crouched on the bench and waited for me to arrive to give him the pickax with which he'd break all the little gods. Everyone is useless around here. Down with the gods! The whole matter could have been settled peacefully if it were not for Henoon, that devil-eye who confessed against me this morning to Nimrod, and who in turn commanded that I be burned.

From behind the bars of my cell in the impregnable castle, I saw them gather wood for the fire, day after day, for the fire that my thin body was to fuel. Then Nimrod came and wrapped me in chains, placed me in a catapult and tossed me into the flames. I wasn't afraid for I knew God would come to rescue me at the last moment as he always did. I even refused when the angel of water offered to open the spout of his clouds to put out my blazing fire. And the guardian of the wind returned defeated and downcast dragging his storms and tempests behind him. Swimming in space, and before my feet touched the hellish flames, I heard the command sounded, coming from the end of creation: O *fire be cool and peaceful on Abraham*. I breathed a sigh of relief confident of my survival. The fire rising to the roof of the sky became a gushing spring in a garden of roses and narcissus flowers. I strolled its every corner for seven days and seven nights, its luxuriant trees shading me. The angel of shade, my look-alike who came to entertain me in my solitude, walked beside me and told me the most beautiful episodes of my life.

Ah, it wouldn't have hurt me to remain there a thousand years!
It wouldn't have hurt me if they gathered all the world's wood to burn me!

from *Bedouins Under an Alien Sky*

(2002)

THE LION AND THE APOSTLE

If you are an apostle whose name is carved in the martyrs' tablet,
I'm the ferocious lion standing before you in the ring.
Dream as you wish of the gardens of Paradise
as I gnaw your limbs to the bone.
Ah, don't damn me. You know that we two,
together,
only play the roles assigned to us in this world.
So rise happy and victorious toward the sky of immortality
while we, lions of the jungle
remain here roaring upon the earth
devouring the saints . . .

NEWTON'S APPLE

Isaac Newton, who spent
most of his life
observing trees
in public parks,
once saw an apple
fall
to the ground.
He remembered
that what tied him to earth
was not the law of gravity
he'd just accidentally discovered,
but the hope
that the apple would fall
upwards.

NOAH AFTER THE FLOOD

After God rescued Noah from the flood,
he commanded him to plant grapevines in his fields.
Since then mankind has been drinking and misbehaving
until the earth filled with corruption and debauchery.

Dear God, if you wish to drown the earth again,
let me be your new Noah.

ON HALF-DESERTED STREETS WITH PRUFROCK

Let us go then you, T. S. Eliot, and I,
to where black night scratches its back with long fingernails
and walk the fog of half-deserted streets that take us to the past
and lift us to the old spring of time
like poets sitting in funeral parlors
until we return to our dark home
to welcome guests who forgot to come to our sumptuous feast.
Socrates swallowed the poison alone to teach us wisdom,
and Al-Mutanabbi fell dead in the desert
for the ferocious wolves to devour
leaving us his blind glory.
Marx rented his glass house in London to the angels.
We had to spend our days in cheap hotels crowded with prostitutes
in Ealing Broadway,
busy with the gold that became dust in our hands.
I too led X, the hero of my novel, once to Baghdad
to hang himself out in the open from a palm tree
despairing of the world like all of us
after its inhabitants fled to another planet
on flying saucers which they'd prepared for the Day of Doom.

Let us go then you, T. S. Eliot, and I to the masked ball,
dressed like pirates whose ship sank at sea.
Let us stay up all through the night.

The bourgeois women will go happily to and fro there in the hall
speaking with their lovers about true love and all.

What does it matter if you heard the sirens sing from the reef?
Surely they sing for neither you nor me.

Let us go, the two of us
through a night splayed like an opium addict,
enchanted, following our pasts
along the streets

aiming for men who lean upon each other out of boredom,
while the lost, mad bird
chirps on the broken branch
of the forgotten tree.

You know we've given time back its cheap gifts
and sat alone there in the forest.
We watched the idea grow in the kingdom of shade
and eternal time bind with ephemeral time
fearing forgetfulness
until we heard the word speak up at last
and the human voice rises once again for our sake.

Our exile is distant and deep as a river.
But we will never drown,
believing that everything will in the end turn out well,
and the rose itself will be the spring in its entirety
united with fire.

THE SURPRISE

Franz Kafka woke up one morning and found that he was still Franz Kafka: those two hands were his hands, those two legs as well, the head, the face, the mouth, all his. And more importantly, he was still capable of love. He took his breakfast quickly as he did everyday, put on his gray suit and stepped out heading to work.

That's when he saw what shocked him: all the people had turned into big cockroaches crawling from one place to another, forgetting their history, pleased with their new lives. He wanted to escape, but a thousand Gregor Samsas surrounded him from every direction and began to whisper to each other:

From where did this strange cockroach come to our city, and how?

LENIN PLATZ IN BERLIN

There in his square
he stood, arms stretched forward as if begging the passers-by to stop and
      hear him out.
He wore his ragged black coat and had his gray-brown beret pulled over
      his head.
I saw him prophesy revolution to workers
and threaten the bourgeoisie with hell.
He did not even have a chair to sit on;
he remained standing and waited forever.

When they captured him,
he was asleep and dreaming on his high platform.
They cut through his fossilized body with an electric saw
and carried his marble head with a rented crane
to a storeroom of archeological remains.
The workers covered his grassy square with concrete
afraid the thieves of the class struggle would plunder its invaluable dust.

A lot of blood stuck to our shoes
as we walked the streets following his coffin to its final rest.

Dasfedanya!

TOASTING BETRAYED REVOLUTIONS

Leading a train crowded with strange passengers
fleeing to earth from their hotel in a lost paradise,
I unloaded my bags in a metropolis between heaven and hell,
followed meanwhile by all the poets of the world who chased me like
      shadows.
Then suddenly thousands of the forgotten dead
from African jungles,
from Siberia,
or from . . .
or from . . .
began crowding the sidewalks
to greet me, their poet of betrayed revolutions.
But when I stood on the platform under raised red banners
to sing the praises of my people with poems from the severed throats of
      saints
like a guerrilla fighter after victory, descending from a mountain pass
covered with trees,
Satan rose up and began calling,
"Shut up! Shut up!
Don't you remember, poet, when you used to gnaw at your own heart in
      the morning?
And when you used to sip from the cup of blind history in the taverns
      in the evening?
Do you, poet, deny this?"
Long live the poet!
Down with the poet!

Death approached us with knives flashing in the mob's hands
and axes they'd hidden under their coats.
We were certain the butcher would slaughter us before help arrived.
But my friend Rimbaud, returning from the Paris Commune,
and who's familiar with folk rituals,
came out of a bus parked on the street corner
and brought out a barrel of wine and distributed it for free.
We all drank it, toasting the betrayed revolutions

and danced until the dawn of the next wave of mankind
at the end of eternity's night.
Slipping away at last in the darkness,
I saw Satan the betrayer
twiddling his moustache happily
in the weak light of a lantern
singing his story again
to the masses.

BEFORE THE SKY HAD A NAME

Back then before the sky had a name,
before it was borne out of antimatter,
and I was a child like everyone
holding the tip of my caftan between my teeth
and chasing butterflies in the streets,
I saw Tiamet give birth to her many ferocious beasts:
the seven-headed snake,
the giant lion, the frothing wolf, the scorpion man,
the fish-bull, the stone dragon, and the thundering storm.
My father used to take me to see the eternal fire burning away in Baba
   Gurgun.
He wore his blue jump suit which was smeared with petroleum
and I caught the scent of eternity gushing in white pipes
that extend from Ur to H3,
and from Chokur county to Weisseneer Wey in Berlin
crossing its famous wall.
On holidays we used to go to masked balls
to see the bears that lampooned the old Turkoman women returning
from the vegetable market.
Or we'd go to the mausoleums of the ancient saints to listen to the
   magicians tell the story of Murdoch,
the mad man who hit Tiamat with his mighty sword,
split her in two, and made sky and earth out of her body.
And from the blood of her husband Kanjou, whose head he severed
   with a butcher knife
like any criminal chased by the authorities in a thriller,
he created the human race.
Watching the scene from my high platform
I saw all of humanity pass before me:
I saw Noah rowing his ark, crossing the sea toward dry earth,
Al-Mutanabbi standing before the desert flinging his poems at the
   wind,
Homer the blind leading Ulysses to Ithaca,
Garibaldi bombarding the clouds with his artillery,
Napoleon on his horse crossing hell on his way to Corsica,

Alexander the great Macedonian leading his armies on the Silk Road
    returning to holy Babel,
and Judas the traitor and his commercial partners Dh. M. M Inc.
    sounding their instructions
on megaphones usually rented for parades and feast days.
Rimbaud offers me his favorite concubine to enjoy
in the dusty gardens of Eden.
Al-Sayyab sits by the edge of the Buwaib water mill in starving Jaikur
and submits his poetry identity papers to me so that I can redeem him
    on the Day of Judgment.

Many passed before me and disappeared.
Many others drowned in the deluge.
I didn't even hear the chattering of their teeth
on cold nights.

MIRACLE MAKER

I am the magician, agent of lost souls,
the flock and the shepherd,
the dead and the funeral.
I cross the sky to reach earth.
I spoon embers in my palms from the gods' inferno.
And I steal the temple's pearl
from under the pillow of the dying priest
with the fingers of an expert thief.
I am the miracle maker.
I always drink my toast alone
and I go on my way.
That's me.

FEAST IN CANDLELIGHT

Here is the twentieth century
in its long, dim hall
with murderers and conjurers
sitting at its table
in the flickering candlelight
of their victory,
waiting for their meal.
The waiters come out
one by one
from their hidden corners,
balancing dishes of darkness
on their heads
to serve their guests.

They will all drink from the same bottle
and watch the evening fall among the trees.
Parades of drunken soldiers
wave their bloody flags
and march down the street.

Through the window
the moon will soon shine.

When they finish their feast,
we will sit at that same table
and drink the same wine
too.

NOTES ON THE POEMS

Mr. Edouard Luqa's Dilemma: *Faalan* and *mafulan* are two of the metrical feet commonly used in Arabic poetry.

The Opening: Yathrib is the old name of the holy city of Madina. The name change occurred when the prophet Muhammad made his hegira to Yathrib seeking refuge among its people. From then on it became Madinat al-Rasul (The city of the prophet).

Vision on a Bus: "Recite in the name of thine Lord who created thee!" is the first command given by the archangel Gabriel to the prophet Muhammad. It is the first Quran verse revealed to the prophet.

The Prodigal's Return: The Arabic passage is from the Quran, 89:6–10. The following is an approximate translation of its meaning:

> Have you not seen what your Lord has done to the people Aad?
> And to Iram, city of mighty pillars?
> The like of which had never been made.
> And to the Thamud who cut giant stones in the valley?
> And to Pharaoh, lord of the stakes?

Elegy for the Living: Al-Mutanabbi and Abu Aala Al-Maari are medieval Arab poets, considered the most important in classic Arab literature. Maraud Rasa, Al-Jawahiri, and Jawad Salim are important modern Iraqi poets. Abdulqader Al-Gailani is a medieval figure and the most revered Sufi saint. Abu Nawas is a medieval poet who was patronized by the Abbasid court in Baghdad. Baba Karkar is an oil field near Kirkuk. According to the Quran, zaqqum is a fruit that grows in hell and is fed to the damned.

Abraham in the Garden of Fire: In the Quranic story of Abraham, the young prophet preaches to his pagan kin about the one god, but he is shunned by all including his father. He then goes to destroy the statues of his people's gods for which they decide to burn him at the stake. God then commands the fire to be "safe and cool" on Abraham, and he is not burned even as the fires blaze under him.

Noah After the Flood: The last couplet in the poem is inspired by a passage from the work of Jalal ud-din Rumi, the medieval Persian poet.

ACKNOWLEDGMENTS

Thanks to the editors of the following publications in which these poems appeared:

Banipal: Journal of Modern Arab Literature (London): "From an Open Window unto a Dark Street," "The Magi in Our House," "The Widow on Her Balcony," "Newton's Apple," "Lenin Platz in Berlin," and "Feast in Candlelight";
Rattapallax: "Nothing Happens in My Dreams Anymore" and "Movie in a Train Station."

"In the Court of Honor," "Vision on a Bus," "A Man in Memory," "Song of Myself," "Good Morning, God" "The Prodigal Son Returns," and "No Matter How Far" appeared in *Every Well a Joseph Is Weeping* (Quarterly Review of Literature Poetry Book Series, Volume xxxvi) and are printed here with the permission of the publisher.

ABOUT THE AUTHOR

Fadhil Al-Azzawi is one of the leading experimental writers in the Arab world. Born in 1940 in Kirkuk, Iraq, he has published seven volumes of poetry, six novels, three books of criticism and memoir, and several translations of German literary works. Al-Azzawi participated in Iraq's avant-garde Sixties Generation, and his early controversial work was critiqued and lauded with great enthusiasm. In 1976, as the Baathist-controlled regime was tightening its grip on power, Al-Azzawi left Iraq to earn a doctorate in communications studies from Leipzig University. He has worked as a freelance journalist and translator for Arab newspapers and cultural reviews. He is currently a full-time writer living in Berlin.

ABOUT THE TRANSLATOR

Khaled Mattawa is the author of two books of poetry, *Ismailia Eclipse* and *Zodiac of Echoes*. An assistant professor of English and Creative Writing at the University of Michigan, Ann Arbor, Mattawa has translated three volumes of contemporary Arabic poetry and co-edited an anthology of Arab-American literature.

The Lannan Translations Selection Series

Ljuba Merlina Bortolani, *The Siege*

Olga Orozco, *Engravings Torn from Insomnia*

Gérard Martin, *The Hiddenness of the World*

Fadhil Al-Azzawi, *Miracle Maker*

For more on the Lannan Translations Selection Series
visit our Web site:
www. boaeditions.org